Taking Tourette Syndrome To School

by Tira Krueger

Adapted for the
Special Kids in School® series
created by Kim Gosselin

JayJo Books, L.L.C.
Publishing Special Books for Special Kids®

Taking Tourette Syndrome to School
© 2001 JayJo Books, LLC
Edited by Kim Gosselin

Published by
JayJo Books, LLC
A Guidance Channel Company
Publishing Special Books for Special Kids®

JayJo Books is a publisher of books to help teachers, parents, and children cope with chronic illnesses, special needs, and health education in classroom, family, and social settings.

Library of Congress Control Number: 2001087647
ISBN 1-891383-12-4
First Edition
Ninth book in our *Special Kids in School*® series

For information about
Premium and Special Sales, contact:
JayJo Books Special Sales Office
P.O. Box 213
Valley Park, MO 63088-0213
636-861-1331
jayjobooks@aol.com
www.jayjo.com

For all other information, contact:
JayJo Books
A Guidance Channel Company
135 Dupont Street, P.O. Box 760
Plainview, NY 11803-0760
1-800-999-6884
jayjobooks@guidancechannel.com
www.jayjo.com

The opinions in this book are solely those of the author. Medical care is highly individualized and should never be altered without professional medical consultation.

About the Author

Tira Krueger graduated summa cum laude from Trinity University in San Antonio, Texas with a B.A. in Psychology. She earned an M.S. in Behavioral Science from Cameron University in Lawton, Oklahoma. Tira began her work with special needs kids while a senior in college. Her two children live with Tourette Syndrome and Attention Deficit Hyperactivity Disorder. Tira's goal was to write a book to help other children understand, and no longer fear or ridicule, a child's special challenges.

Tira has worked with special education students at the elementary and middle school level. She is currently employed by the city of San Antonio in the Children's Resource Division. This book is Tira's first.

Hello boys and girls! My name is Megan, and I'm a kid living with Tourette Syndrome. Tourette Syndrome is a kind of tic disorder. Having Tourette Syndrome means that my nervous system, the part of my body that helps me move and feel, doesn't always work the way it is supposed to. Because of this, sometimes I might look, act, or sound differently than I normally do.

Everybody has a nervous system, but not everyone has Tourette Syndrome.

Have you ever had an itch you just had to scratch, no matter what? Having Tourette Syndrome is kind of like that. Sometimes I feel like I have to move part of my body. Or, I feel like I have to make a funny sound, like a squeak. These sudden moves and funny sounds are called tics.

Having tics is something I can't help. They are just part of my life.

Doctors and nurses don't know why I have Tourette Syndrome. I didn't do anything wrong, and it's nobody's fault. They do know you can't catch Tourette Syndrome from me or anyone else! It's okay to be my friend and play with me.

I can't give you Tourette Syndrome.

When I have tics, they don't hurt me at all! Sometimes I have to suddenly move my hand or my knee. Sometimes I need to blink my eyes. Other times I need to cough or make funny sounds. Tics might happen to me many times during the day, or they might hardly ever happen. There are medicines I can take to help my nervous system relax, so my tics don't happen as often.

When I take my medicine, I feel much better. It's nice to feel relaxed!

When I feel tired or get very nervous, I usually have more tics. Sometimes I get embarrassed about my tics, so please don't tease me or make fun of me.

When people tease me about my tics, I feel sad.

My tics can make some things hard for me. If I have a tic in my hand, it might make it hard for me to write my spelling words. If I have to blink my eyes a lot, it can make it hard for me to read my assignments. My muscles might even get sore if I have a lot of tics.

Having tics is not easy. Sometimes I have to work extra hard at my schoolwork.

If I have a tic in my face, it might look like I'm making funny faces or winking at you. Remember, I can't help my tics. I never do them on purpose. Having tics is not fun!

I didn't do anything wrong to cause my tics, and it's nobody's fault either!

When I make funny sounds, they are called vocal tics. They might be words or sounds that I repeat a lot. Sometimes the sounds are loud. This can be a problem when I'm supposed to be quiet, like during a test. I might need to leave the classroom if my tics are bothering other students. I'm not leaving because I'm in trouble though!

Remember, tics are just something my body needs to do. They are nothing to be afraid of.

There are days when my tics are better and days when my tics are worse. Nobody really knows why. If I'm feeling relaxed, I usually don't have as many tics. It helps if I get plenty of rest and exercise.

Of course, these are good habits for everyone!

Like most kids, I love to play at recess and take part in gym class. My tics might start when I play certain kinds of games. Please be patient with me, and you will help me to relax. If I relax, I usually have fewer tics.

Having Tourette Syndrome doesn't stop me from doing anything other kids do!

Maybe someday there will be a cure for Tourette Syndrome and other tic disorders. That means doctors and nurses will be able to make them go away! Even if this doesn't happen, please don't treat me any differently just because I have Tourette Syndrome.

After all, nobody's perfect. In fact, I bet I'm a lot like you in almost every other way!

LET'S TAKE THE
TOURETTE SYNDROME KIDS' QUIZ!

1. **What part of my body causes me to have tics?**
   My nervous system.

2. **Can you catch Tourette Syndrome (or another tic disorder) from me?**
   No! Tourette Syndrome is not contagious.
   It's okay to be my friend and play with me.

3. **Did I do anything wrong to cause me to have Tourette Syndrome?**
   No, and it's nobody else's fault either!

4. **What are the tics called when I make sounds?**
   Vocal tics.

5. **Should you treat me any differently just because I have a tic disorder?**
   No. Remember, I'm a lot like you in every other way!

   Great job! Thanks for taking the Tourette Syndrome Kids' Quiz!

TEN TIPS FOR TEACHERS

✓ **1. CHILDREN LIVING WITH TOURETTE SYNDROME (OR OTHER TIC DISORDERS) ARE DIFFERENT FROM EACH OTHER.**

Some children have only motor tics, which are sudden movements. These can include blinking, nose wrinkling, shoulder shrugging or hand movements. Some kids have only vocal tics such as squeaking, grunting, sniffing or coughing. Kids with Tourette Syndrome usually have both kinds of tics. Their tics vary in frequency and severity from day to day. Stressful situations such as a test or speaking in front of the class will often make tics worse.

✓ **2. THE CHILD'S OVERACTIVE NERVOUS SYSTEM CAUSES THE SYMPTOMS OF TOURETTE SYNDROME AND OTHER TIC DISORDERS.**

Tourette Syndrome has no effect on intelligence or learning ability. However, more than half of children with Tourette Syndrome also have a co-existing disorder, such as Attention Deficit Disorder. These conditions will not always be diagnosed at the same time. Your observations, however, will be valuable in helping students get all the assistance they need to reach their full potential.

✓ **3. IGNORE MYTHS YOU MAY HAVE HEARD ABOUT TOURETTE SYNDROME.**

While it is true that some people with Tourette Syndrome have outbursts of inappropriate language, these kids make up fewer than ten percent of all cases. The majority of people with Tourette Syndrome have only mild to moderate symptoms. Tourette Syndrome can often be well controlled through medication. Kids with tics display social problems mainly because of embarrassment or feeling different. You can help them feel more comfortable.

✓ **4. DON'T PUNISH THE STUDENT FOR LIVING WITH TOURETTE SYNDROME.**

A child can have Tourette Syndrome, or any other tic disorder, for years before it is recognized, properly diagnosed, and treated. Since children with tic disorders can suppress their tics for short periods of time, it is often assumed they are making the movements and sounds on purpose. While tics can be annoying to others, imagine what it must be like for the person needing to express the tics!

✓ **5. SET CLEAR LIMITS THAT DON'T ALLOW TEASING OR IMITATING THE STUDENT.**

Children are naturally curious about differences. They may attempt to imitate a child's tics. They may ask a student why he keeps making a specific sound or movement. This book can be part of the education process for other students in the classroom. The child with a tic disorder must be protected from ridicule and teasing. Please help them any way you can.

6. PROVIDE INCONSPICUOUS GUIDANCE TO BALANCE DIFFERING NEEDS.

There may be times tics are so disruptive that the student needs to leave the classroom temporarily. You and the student might agree upon a code word that lets the child go into the hall to express tics without disturbing other students. This agreement must be handled delicately and coordinated with the parents and caregivers. It should never appear to be punishment.

7. RECESS AND PHYSICAL ACTIVITY CAN CALM THE NERVOUS SYSTEM AND RELIEVE THE NEED FOR A CHILD WITH TOURETTE SYNDROME TO DISPLAY TICS.

Ideally, the student living with Tourette Syndrome will have full recess and physical education privileges. It is important to check with other members of your student's treatment team to make sure this is possible.

8. CONSIDER YOURSELF PART OF YOUR STUDENT'S TEAM.

Expect to work with the parents, medical professionals, school nurse, and other caregivers. The child with a tic disorder may take one or more medications daily. Some of these may have side effects such as sleepiness. New medications may be introduced, and various combinations of medicines may be tried. It is important to communicate with parents so you know what to expect. Work as a team!

9. BE PATIENT.

Students with Tourette Syndrome may have frequent doctor visits. Allow them time to make up schoolwork. Some tics, such as eye blinking, may interfere with reading. Other children have hand movement tics that can interfere with their writing. Some days, tics will be barely noticeable. Other days the child may have tics every few seconds, which is frustrating and tiring. Your attitude will help set the tone for others' reactions to these challenges.

10. A CHILD WITH A TIC DISORDER IS NO DIFFERENT THAN OTHER STUDENTS IN YOUR CLASSROOM.

All children are unique and may have various difficulties to cope with. While a tic disorder is certainly more visible than many other problems or conditions, your student needs to feel accepted and normal. He or she wants to be considered a contributing member of the class. Allow the child to be so, and you both will be rewarded greatly.

ADDITIONAL RESOURCES

Tourette Syndrome Association, Inc.
42-40 Bell Boulevard
Bayside, NY 11361-2820
718-224-2999
www.tsa-usa.org

**National Institute of
Neurological Disorders and Stroke**
NIH Neurological Institute
P.O. Box 5801
Bethesda, MD 20824
800-352-9424
www.ninds.nih.gov

Tourette Syndrome Online
3139 West Holcombe Blvd.
Suite 265
Houston, TX 77025
www.tourette-syndrome.com

Tourette Syndrome "Plus"
www.tourettesyndrome.net

Touretter ... Because TS Kids Can Help Each Other
http://pub23.ezboard.com/btskidsabulletinboardwhe

To order additional copies of *Taking Tourette Syndrome to School* or inquire about our quantity discounts for schools, hospitals, and affiliated organizations, contact us at 1-800-999-6884.

From our *Special Kids in School*® series

Taking A.D.D. to School
Taking Asthma to School
Taking Autism to School
Taking Cancer to School
Taking Cerebral Palsy to School
Taking Cystic Fibrosis to School
Taking Diabetes to School
Taking Food Allergies to School
Taking Seizure Disorders to School
... and others coming soon!

From our new *Healthy Habits for Kids*™ series

There's a Louse in My House
A Fun Story about Kids and Head Lice

Coming soon ...
Playtime Is Exercise!
A Fun Story about Exercise and Play

From our new *Special Family and Friends*™ series

Allie Learns about Alzheimer's Disease
A Family Story about Love, Patience, and Acceptance
... and others coming soon!

Other books available now!

SPORTSercise!
A School Story about Exercise-Induced Asthma

ZooAllergy
A Fun Story about Allergy and Asthma Triggers

Rufus Comes Home
Rufus the Bear with Diabetes™
A Story about Diagnosis and Acceptance

The ABC's of Asthma
An Asthma Alphabet Book for Kids of All Ages

Taming the Diabetes Dragon
A Story about Living Better with Diabetes

Trick-or-Treat for Diabetes
A Halloween Story for Kids Living with Diabetes

And from our *Substance Free Kids*® series

Smoking STINKS!! ™
A Heartwarming Story about the Importance of Avoiding Tobacco

A portion of the proceeds from all our publications is donated to various charities to help fund important medical research and education. We work hard to make a difference in the lives of children with chronic conditions and/or special needs. Thank you for your support.